SECOND EDITION

Designing your first
RESEARCH
PROPOSAL

A manual for
beginning researchers

SECOND EDITION

Designing your first
RESEARCH
PROPOSAL

A manual for
beginning researchers

**Renuka Vithal &
Jonathan Jansen**

JUTA

Designing your first research proposal — A manual for beginning researchers

First published 1997
Reprinted 2002
Reprinted 2003
Reprinted 2004
Reprinted 2006
Revised reprint 2010
Second edition 2019

PO Box 14373, Lansdowne 779, Cape Town, South Africa

Juta & Company Ltd
21 Dreyer Street
First Floor, Sunclare Building
Claremont
Cape Town
7708

www.juta.co.za

© 2019 Juta & Company Ltd

ISBN 978 1 48512 990 5
WebPDF 978 1 48512 991 2

Project manager: Mmakasa Ramoshaba
Typesetter: LT Design Worx
Cover designer: Genevieve Simpson
Proofreader: Edith Viljoen

Published in South Africa

Contents

Preface

This book – or, more precisely, research manual – first emerged from our joint experience in the training of Masters and Doctoral students in the field of science and mathematics education. In the course of our teaching on how to think about and do social and educational research, we learnt volumes from our postgraduate students about what 'works' in the design and execution of competent research. We listened carefully to their expectations, their fears and their initial experiences of putting together research proposals and testing them in the field. Out of these teaching and learning experiences we discovered that there were powerful ways of making this, often intimidating, task – writing your first research proposal – accessible and meaningful to beginning researchers.

The workshop format of our training model proceeded on the basis of three simple commitments:

1. Each participant would over the course of the training develop an actual research proposal in a step-wise manner as outlined in this manual – starting with the statement of purpose and then moving to the research question(s) and so on.
2. Each participant would provide honest but supportive feedback on the research proposals of their peers in the workshop; in other words, the participants shared responsibility for the progress of the group.
3. Each participant would develop a research proposal that was do-able (realistic as a research plan), defendable (justifiable on academic grounds) and fundable (capable of attracting financial resources for putting the plan into action).

The demands for these workshops increased across the country and we decided to translate the rich workshop content and experiences into a user-friendly research manual which could be used by academic supervisors, mentors, and by individual or groups of postgraduate students.

This edition of *Designing your first research proposal* has been updated based on new knowledge in the field of research; expanded to include more diverse and contemporary examples from education and the social sciences; and corrected to deal with missing elements in earlier editions such as the ethics and funding of research. We were careful in making these changes not to change the basic format of this manual as a simple-to-use, practical guide for putting together your research proposal.

 # Acknowledgements

We gratefully acknowledge the invaluable inputs of the following persons on successive drafts of this research manual: Professor Ole Skovsmose and the late Mr David Brookes. Special thanks are due to the participants from the workshops that laid the basis for the development of this manual. We thank, in particular, Farida Patel, a participant in the first workshop, for allowing us to use notes taken during the workshop.

 # Some guidelines for the effective use of this manual

1. This manual offers a practical, application-focused, illustrated guide to writing a research proposal.

2. This manual should not be read as a blueprint for designing research proposals. Research design, like fashion design or curriculum design, is a creative process which reflects the personal tastes and preferences of the designer, cost considerations, the time available, the audience, and the many other factors which shape design decisions.

3. This manual is not a substitute for more intensive theoretical and methodological engagement with the many issues pertinent to research design and proposal writing. It does, however, attempt to provide a simple, clear and coherent strategy for preparing a research proposal without getting lost in the thicket of issues or the specialist language which often intimidates new researchers.

4. This manual could serve various purposes and audiences: it could be used by beginner researchers; research supervisors; research training specialists; or teachers involved in classroom-based research (such as action research). It could be used as a guide to design a research proposal for funding or a dissertation proposal for university approval, or to prepare a proposal for independent research.

5. This manual is best used in a research training context; by a skilled and experienced facilitator; working systematically through the manual; with a group of participants in dialogue on the issues raised in each section of the manual.

6. This manual is designed in such a way that it not only illustrates a set of steps in research design but also generates the kinds of questions which all researchers should ask when evaluating a research proposal.

7. The Appendices to this manual provide examples of actual research instruments that demonstrate how different parts of the process come together in exemplary designs.

8. This manual includes 'work boxes' in each section so that researchers can immediately and progressively complete the details of their proposals as they work through the manual. When these work boxes have been systematically filled in, they collectively provide a first draft outline of the researcher's actual proposal.

9. It must be emphasised that this manual should not be read literally as a linear sequence of neat and tidy steps in the research process. There are many points of entry into research. Some disciplines, such as legal scholarship or pharmaceutical research, have particular modes of inquiry and analysis in research. The research process invariably moves back and forth between problem, method, and analysis. For instance, a research problem might only become clearer during the course of planning the research process.

10. It should be noted that different disciplines or institutions may refer to the key components of the research proposal using a variety of different terminology. For example, a 'data collection plan' may be referred to as a 'research protocol'.

11. While the concept of a 'research proposal manual' attempts to make the process of planning research clearer and simpler, it cannot account for the complexity and unpredictability of the research process.

12. Finally, we encourage users of this manual to constantly reflect on ways of adapting the manual for research training in their particular contexts of teaching and learning about research. This manual should be used flexibly and critically. It is not a recipe for doing research but one of many critical tools that help to make sense of the exciting world of research.

 # Steps in writing a research proposal

Research proposals are often organised around the following activities:

1. Selecting a focus

2. Identifying critical questions

3. Stating a rationale

4. Conducting a literature review

5. Locating a theoretical framework

6. Preparing a data collection plan

7. Planning for data analysis

8. Anticipating the report outline

9. Dealing with validity and reliability concerns

10. Acknowledging the limitations of the research

11. Protecting human subjects (ethics)

12. Estimating the budget

These steps are not sequential in the real world of research. For example, critical questions may be refined following initial research findings, and data collection plans are often modified based on problems anticipated with data analysis. However, being clear about the different tasks in research design facilitates the planning and preparation of a research proposal.

Section 1
Selecting a focus

A first step in the research design process could be deciding on a FOCUS for your research. This may take the form of a 'statement of purpose'.

Examples of 'statements of purpose':

> The purpose of this study is to explain the poor performance of students in high school mathematics.

> The purpose of this study is to investigate the attitudes of student teachers towards the use of corporal punishment in schools.

> The purpose of this study is to examine how the use of social media in the home impacts on family relationships.

Now write a sentence which describes your statement of purpose by completing the following sentence, using not more than ten words:

The purpose of this study is to ...

Consider the following 'WEAK' examples of 'statements of purpose'. In each example write down why you think it could be considered to be a weak statement of purpose.

Statement of purpose	Reason
... to prove that the science curriculum is racist.	
... to visit municipal offices in Soweto.	
... to investigate problems of three-way misconceptions among black, Catholic, vegetarian females suffering from dyslexia in the Matubatuba district of North Eastern KwaZulu-Natal primary schools, with special reference to learning theories in geometry.	

See Appendix A, A.1, for reasons why these might be considered 'weak' statements of purpose for a research design.

Consider the following 'GOOD' examples of 'statements of purpose'. In each example write down why you think it could be considered to be a good statement of purpose. Also identify the common features in these statements.

Statement of purpose	Reason
... to assess the impact of the new history curriculum on learners taught by underqualified teachers in primary schools.	
... to measure the social rates of return on investment in higher education.	
... to explore the reasons for campus suicides among student survivors.	

... to document the experiences of women executives in high-tech industries.	
... to compare the ways in which novice and experienced teachers teach science in under-resourced classrooms.	

See Appendix A, A.2, for reasons why these could be considered exemplary statements of purpose for a research design.

Learning points

1. A broad distinction often made in research is between QUANTITATIVE (for example, statistical or experimental studies) and QUALITATIVE (for example, biographical narratives or case studies) research. Which of the five statements in the 'good' examples section would you classify as being more appropriate for quantitative or qualitative research?

2. When key words or phrases such as 'to determine' appear in statements of purpose, they often suggest that quantitative research approaches may be more appropriate; whereas 'to explore' or 'to understand' suggest that the study may be qualitative in nature.

3. A statement of purpose for a specific study does more than just impart a research focus; it also hints at the way in which that study may be carried out, for example using mainly quantitative or qualitative methods.

4. Note that the statement of purpose should be distinguished from the title of the study, which is usually shorter and may be a 'catchy' phrase or a provocative question. The focus statement clearly, precisely and specifically expresses the researcher's purpose.

Notes:

Section 2
Identifying critical questions

Having selected the focus of your research in the previous section, the next step could be to identify CRITICAL QUESTIONS which further refine your broad statement of purpose.

Examples of critical questions for a given statement of purpose:

Statement of purpose:
To investigate the use of new science materials by primary school teachers.

Critical questions:
1. What do teachers value in the use of the new materials?

2. How do teachers use the materials differently in different contexts?

3. Why do teachers use the materials differently in different classroom contexts?

Observe that the following criteria have been taken into account when identifying these critical questions:

*   All three questions relate directly to the statement of purpose.

*   Each question is linked logically to the other two questions; for example, you can only answer question 3 if you have already answered 2.

*   Each question is linked conceptually to the other questions through the key term(s) which appear in each question. In the example, each question has to do with 'the use of materials' by teachers.

*   Each question can stand on its own as a researchable question; each question is also self-explanatory and clear to an outside reader.

Now examine your statement of purpose and write down three critical research questions relevant to the focus of your study:

Statement of purpose:

Critical question 1:

Critical question 2:

Critical question 3:

Learning points

1. Of course, it is possible to develop any number of critical questions. We propose three questions for the purposes of this manual as a way of retaining a sharp focus on what you, as a researcher, intend to do by remaining focused on a limited number of issues. Our experience is that novice researchers often develop long, unmanageable lists of questions for research. While such lists may be useful at an exploratory stage, they need to be captured in a realistic research plan. You may find that the questions may merge, fall away or expand when you begin to develop your data collection strategies. You may end up with more or fewer than three questions.

2. As with the statement of purpose, keep the questions simple and concise in order to stay focused.

3. When formulating the critical questions, ensure that they relate directly and exclusively to what has been outlined in the statement of purpose.

Notes:

Section 3
Stating a rationale

A RATIONALE usually serves as a succinct statement of:

- how the researcher came to develop an interest in the proposed topic

- why the researcher believes the proposed research is worth doing.

Below is an example of a rationale developed by an educational researcher working with second language English students:

> Since starting as an English teacher two years ago, I noticed that second language (L2) learners display a distinct difference in their ability to speak English (which they do well) and write in English (which they do poorly). I decided to investigate the possible reasons for this disjunction between spoken and written English among L2 speakers. The findings from this research could be useful to:
>
> - teachers of L2 learners with an interest in improving the writing skills of students
>
> - curriculum development specialists and textbook writers who prepare English material for L2 classrooms
>
> - L2 researchers who might wish to test the findings with non-English L2 learning contexts, for example Afrikaans or isiZulu.

Observe that the researcher explains how she became interested in the topic in terms of personal experiences based on a puzzle or paradox. Other ways in which researchers develop an interest in a research topic include:

- a gap or silence in the research literature

- an untested theory

- involvement in collective, funded research

- dissatisfaction with an existing practice or belief.

Note that in the above example the justification for the research (that is, why the research is worth doing) is framed in terms of:

- teachers
- curriculum or material development specialists
- policymakers.

Now write a rationale for your research:

Rationale for the study:

Learning points

1. The rationale should be brief and to the point. Avoid long background descriptions which are not immediately relevant to the research question(s).

2. The rationale can be written in the first person singular. In our view, this allows for greater personal engagement with the topic than does a distant, impersonal writing style which often impedes authentic descriptions of the research. However, different journals, institutions and research supervisors may have their own expectations on this issue.

3. The significance of any study is usually articulated in terms of its contribution to improving practice, informing policy or enriching the knowledge base on the topic or issue being investigated.

4. The significance of a study that is stated in terms of advancing knowledge of a subject (for example second language learning) is a powerful justification for doing your investigation. However, this means that you should have a thorough grasp of what the existing research says (or does not say) about that topic.

Notes:

Section 4

Conducting a literature review

A LITERATURE REVIEW offers a synthesis of:

- what has already been written on the topic

- what has not been written on that topic, or is written in such a way that it is conceptually or methodologically inadequate, with the goal of clarifying

- how the researcher's proposal addresses the 'gap', silence or weakness in the existing literature.

Here is an example of a brief excerpt from a literature review on the topic of effective schools:

The existing research on effective schools has been based on:

1.　'input–output' models applied to

2.　large survey studies (50 or more schools) of

3.　American and British schools.

The literature is therefore limited in that it fails to:

- pinpoint the in-school processes or transactions which make schools effective or ineffective or

- offer in-depth descriptions of a few schools or

- explain school effectiveness in developing countries.

My research will therefore provide detailed case studies of five effective schools in southern Africa with a focus on the processes or interactions within schools and classrooms which explain 'effectiveness'.

Observe that the researcher uses three limitations in the existing literature on effective schools to justify her research focus:

1. a methodological limitation – using large survey studies

2. a contextual limitation – applied only in British and American schools

3. a conceptual limitation – using input–output studies.

What are some other kinds of limitations which could be uncovered by a literature review?

Now briefly outline a possible literature review for your study; that is, what possible literature would you look for on your topic?

Is it possible for you to identify, at this stage, possible limitations in this literature?

Literature review for the study:

Learning points

1. A literature review is an informed assessment of the existing research on the topic under study.

2. It demonstrates that the researcher has read extensively and intensively on the topic. This is indispensable for the credibility of a well-written, informed literature review, which is expected to include relevant, recent and seminal writings.

3. A literature review is a critical synthesis of the existing research, not an open-ended, long-winded description of 'who said what'.

4. A literature review is goal-focused. The goal is to identify limitations in the existing research on a subject in order to justify the proposed research.

5. In preparing for a literature review, progressively narrow down your reading of the literature as close to the topic as possible.

Notes:

Section 5

Locating a conceptual/ theoretical framework

A CONCEPTUAL or THEORETICAL FRAMEWORK could be described as a well-developed, coherent explanation for an event; for example, Piaget's theory of child development or Bandura's social learning theory.

Researchers may specify a theoretical framework for the following reasons:

- to locate their research – that is, to signal where the research is coming from

- to test a theory – that is, to assess the validity of a theory's propositions in the study being undertaken

- to compare the explanatory power of two rival theories

- to apply a theory – that is, to use a theory's propositions in the design and conduct of the study.

Here is an example of an excerpt from a theoretical framework:

> This research is informed by Piaget's theory of development, which holds that children progress through discrete stages of intellectual development. While working within the Piagetian framework, this research will also explore the validity of this developmental theory in:
>
> - developing-country contexts
>
> - using intellectual tasks different from those originally assigned when the theory was developed.

Does the above example test, apply, or merely 'locate' the proposed research within established theory?

What is the difference between a theoretical framework and a typical literature review?

Briefly describe a theoretical framework which may apply in your study, and explain how it will be used in your research:

Theoretical framework:

Learning points

1. A theory is selected for its power and elegance in explaining an educational or social event, for example why children fail. It is not used for ornamental purposes in a study.

2. A theory is also a perspective on events and always exists in the context of competing or rival theories.

3. A 'conceptual framework' can be distinguished from a 'theoretical framework' in that it is a less well-developed explanation for events. For example, it might link two or three key concepts or principles without being developed into a full-blown theory.

4. Often the terms 'conceptual framework' and 'theoretical framework' are used interchangeably (as if they were the same thing).

5. Considering the 'conceptual' or 'theoretical' framework in a study assists in making assumptions built into the research explicit.

6. To select a theoretical framework requires familiarity with new and established theories in the proposed area of research.

7. Note that a literature review can sometimes review key concepts within a field of study in such a way that the review constitutes a conceptual framework for the study. Similarly, a theoretical framework could emerge from a literature review of relevant theories on a given subject.

8. Not all studies require explicit theoretical frameworks. For example, they may not be needed in explorations of new areas of research where well-developed theories do not yet exist.

9. In new areas of research or where theories are not available, 'grounded theory' can be used to generate theory from data that is carefully collected and analysed. The researcher therefore does not start with a theory and apply it (deductive), but rather the theory is built up from the data (inductive). This is not easy to do for a novice researcher.

Notes:

Section 6
Preparing a data collection plan

A DATA COLLECTION PLAN sets out in detail a strategy for collecting data. Typically, the description of a data collection plan includes the following elements:

- the general methodological strategy
- the research parameters within which the data will be collected
- the research instruments.

1. The data collection plan is often preceded by a statement about the *general methodological strategy*.

Some examples are:

> This research presents *case studies* of racial integration at former white South African high schools.

> This research undertakes a *comparative analysis* of the concept of grief in different cultures.

Now try to formulate a similar statement about the methodological orientation for your research:

This research ...

2. A second step is for the researcher to develop a detailed data collection plan which sets out the *parameters* for each of the identified critical questions. By 'parameters' we mean decisions about what data to collect, from whom, how often, etc.

Before defining the parameters, it is important to recognise the *multiplicity of sources* for data collection.

Consider the following sources of data which could be used in research to address a particular research question:

surveys	documents	records	adverts
photographs	journals	interviews	census data
oral history	questionnaires	cases	buildings
garbage	audio tapes	body language	drawings
biographies	music	tests	posters
written work	stamps	letters	excavations
observations	videos	furniture	statistics
accidents	dialogue	conferences	critical incidents
articles in news media	playgrounds	lectures	minutes of meetings

Add some others:

List sources of data for your study:

Here is an example of a strategy for data collection:

Critical question: How do teachers use the new science textbook?

Questions for developing a data collection plan	A data collection plan
WHY is the data being collected?	to determine how teachers *intend to use* the textbook (that is, before) and how they *actually use* the textbook in the science classroom (that is, after)
WHAT is the research strategy?	*interviews* will be conducted to collect the required data
WHO (or what) will be the sources of the data?	*science teachers* will be interviewed
WHERE is the data to be collected?	the science teachers will be interviewed at *primary schools in Umbumhulu*
HOW MANY of the data sources will be accessed?	*six* science teachers will be interviewed, two from each of three primary schools
HOW OFTEN will data be collected?	the teachers will be interviewed *once before a lesson* (to collect data about teacher intention) and *once after their lesson* (to collect data about actual usage)
HOW will the data be collected?	data will be collected through *semi-structured interviews* which will be *recorded*
JUSTIFY this plan for data collection. (Why is this the best way of collecting data for this critical question?)	The interviews will provide the most direct evidence of teacher intentions and usage of the textbook. They will be semi-structured to allow the researcher to probe initial responses. The six teachers at the three schools represent all teachers who have agreed to participate in the research.

Now complete the same table above using classroom observations (rather than interviews) of the teachers' use of the textbook.

Using the guidelines set out above, complete the following table for one of the critical questions you have identified for your own research.

Critical question:

Questions	Your data collection plan
WHY is the data being collected?	
WHAT is the research strategy?	
WHO (or what) will be the sources of the data?	
WHERE is the data to be collected?	
HOW MANY of the data sources will be accessed?	
HOW OFTEN will data be collected?	
HOW will the data be collected?	
JUSTIFY this plan for data collection.	

3.   The next step in the data collection plan is to design the *research instruments*.

Consider the research instrument in the given example which required the development of an *interview schedule* to be used by a researcher to interview the teachers *after* they had used the textbook in class.

Example of a semi-structured interview schedule:

Critical research question: How do primary school teachers use the new science textbooks? (assume every child also received a copy of the new science textbook)

Interview schedule questions:

- How did you plan to introduce the new textbook to the children?

- How did you plan to use the textbook in your teaching?

- Could you use the textbook as planned? In other words, did you make any changes to your initial plan once you started the actual teaching?

- Did you also use other textbooks in your planning? If so, why?

- What did the new textbook offer that was different from other textbooks when it comes to science teaching?

- Did you use the new textbook primarily as a general resource for teaching or as the main text to guide every step of your teaching?

- Did the new textbook help or hinder you in teaching the topics and concepts in the official science curriculum? Explain.

- Do you use the textbook primarily for planning lessons or for actual work in the classroom or for homework assignments?

- How would you recommend other teachers use the new science textbook based on your own experience?

- How did the children respond to the use of the textbook during your teaching? (Prompts: enjoyment; boredom; confusion; understanding; participation)

Observe the following:

- Every *interview question* is directly related to the *research question*.

- There is a difference between a *research question* (the broad question of interest) and the *interview questions* (the specific questions you ask the respondent).

See Appendix B for examples of other types of research instruments, such as:
- observation schedules
- profiles
- interview schedules
- questionnaires.

Now develop a draft design of a research instrument for one of your critical questions:

Critical question:

_____

_____

_____

_____

Research instrument:

_____

_____

_____

_____

_____

_____

_____

_____

_____

_____

_____

_____

_____

_____

_____

Learning points

1. Be creative and innovative when planning data collection.

2. Any data collection procedure will have advantages and limitations.

3. It is important to be able to justify your choice of research strategy.

4. Maintain a close link between the critical questions and the research strategy.

5. Different research questions often require different choices of instruments.

6. Developing an appropriate research strategy requires more than simply a 'method' in a narrow, instrumentalist sense.

7. Research instruments may be:
   - developed from scratch
   - existing instruments
   - modified from existing instruments.

8. Instruments, for example questionnaires, are often piloted with representatives similar to the sample in the study to check for clarity and meaningfulness of questions, or can reviewed by a reference group which includes researchers from different disciplinary or research backgrounds.

9. More than one strategy/source may be used in collecting data for a particular research question. Data from a variety of sources/instruments, such as a combination of interviews and observations, assist in providing the necessary checks and balances in the research (see the section on validity).

Notes:

Planning for data analysis

Having collected the data from the field, the purpose of DATA ANALYSIS is to make sense of the accumulated information.

Data analysis includes at least three steps:

- Scanning and cleaning the data

- Organising the data

- Presenting the data.

1. *Scanning and cleaning the data* requires the researcher to prepare the raw data for analysis by:

   - reading the data

   - checking for incomplete, inaccurate, inconsistent or irrelevant data

   - identifying preliminary trends in the scanned data to facilitate the organisation of the data into meaningful 'chunks'.

2. *Organising the data* allows the researcher to make sense of the information by arranging it in a manageable form. This may require the researcher to:

   - **count:** for example, how many teachers 'strongly agreed' on a limited-choice, 5-point item in a questionnaire

   - **describe:** for example, descriptions which provide in-depth analytic (as opposed to journalistic) descriptive narratives about a sequence of events – for instance describing how teachers interact with learners in project work

   - **compare:** for example, responses from different students on a test item

   - **categorise:** for example, by identifying patterns of responses on a question or embedded themes; through the use of descriptive statistics (for example averages and means); or through the use of inferential statistics (for example regression analysis).

3. *Presenting the data* in different ways often provides meaningful summaries of large amounts of data. This can take several forms:

- **tables:** for example, cross-tabulations

- **graphs:** for example, pie charts (which show relationships of parts to the whole); histograms (which show comparisons between categories); line graphs (which emphasise time and rate of change); and scatter graphs (which demonstrate trends and patterns)

- **statistical summaries:** for example, means; standard deviations; correlations; and results of other statistical procedures

- **selected quotations:** for example, powerful, representative or illustrative direct statements from responses to a question in an interview

- **case boxes:** an example of which appears below:

Primary science teaching – composing a narrative from observational data

The science teacher in this rural primary classroom was conducting an experiment. The two burning candles were covered by a small jar in the one case and a larger jar in the other case. The students watched carefully. As expected the flame from the candle under the smaller jar went out first and, a few minutes later, the flame from the larger jar was also extinguished. This was the first ever practical demonstration of a science experiment in this poor, rural school. The teacher should be applauded. Except she did all the talking. She told students what was happening. In the one instance where she asked the children to explain what happened, she gave the answer even before a hand could be raised. The very essence of science – doing and thinking and querying and debating – was lost in the teacher-dominated lesson.

> # Learning points
>
> 1. The actual steps taken in a data analysis strategy may differ according to the type of data and the nature of the research (qualitative or quantitative).
>
> 2. Data collection and data analysis is an iterative process; that is, the researcher moves repeatedly back and forth through the data (collecting–analysing–collecting–analysing) rather than in a simple, linear direction.
>
> 3. Most data analysis procedures, especially in larger studies, utilise computer-based software programs, whether such studies are qualitative (for example Atlas.ti) or quantitative (for example SPSS) in nature.

Discuss a plan for analysing the data collected in your study:

Plan for data analysis in the study:

Anticipating the report outline

A REPORT OUTLINE suggests the way in which the research report or dissertation will be divided into chapters or sections. It is a preliminary document.

Here is an example of a conventional report outline:

TITLE (provisional)

1. Purpose of study

2. Critical questions

3. Rationale

4. Literature review

5. Theoretical (or conceptual) framework

6. Methodology

7. Critical question 1
   7.1 Re-statement of the critical question
   7.2 Summarising the data collection and analysis for this critical question
   7.3 Specifying and discussing the research findings related to this critical question

8. Critical question 2 (and so on)

9. Discussion of overall research findings
   9.1 The general research findings
   9.2 The significance of the research findings
   9.3 The limitations of the research

10. References

11. Appendices, for example instrumentation, other documents

Learning points

1. There are many creative ways to organise the research report; the illustrative example is one conventional way of planning and writing a thesis or dissertation which captures the main components of a research report.

2. The illustration assumes that the researcher has two critical questions: you may have more or less.

3. The report outline at this stage is a preliminary and tentative sketch of what the final report could look like. In reality, the report may look very different after two to five years of research. However, such an initial outline is a useful planning tool for the researcher and an important way of communicating the research plan to an external audience, such as a dissertation committee.

Now write out your provisional report outline but write in the actual title and critical questions in the relevant chapter headings. Feel free to transform the critical question into a different 'chapter heading' statement.

Report outline for the study:

Title:

Dealing with validity and reliability concerns

Validity

How does a researcher know that he or she read something?

Validity is an attempt to 'check out' whether the meaning and interpretation of an event is sound or whether a particular measure is an accurate reflection of what you observed.

Consider, for example, the following event, adapted from an example used by the anthropologist, Clifford Geertz:

There are several people in a room. Rajesh enters the room and winks in the direction of Lindiwe.

Possible interpretations of this event may include:

- Rajesh is greeting Lindiwe

- Rajesh is making a pass at/flirting with Lindiwe

- Rajesh is communicating some message to Lindiwe

- Rajesh has an eye irritation.

How will the observer (researcher) know what the winking of the eye actually means?

The data about this event may be collected by:

a) interviewing Rajesh
    interviewing Lindiwe
    interviewing some/all the other people in the room and

b) comparing the meanings articulated by the different respondents.

The researcher may strengthen the validity of (qualitative) research by:

1. Using more than one source of data (such as observations, interviews, document analysis) to check whether what you find is accurate (triangulation).

2. Deploying more than one researcher to observe the same event to check whether what you see or find is accurate (peer debriefing).

3. Keeping a list or an account of everything you did in the course of doing the research so that it is easy to go back and check whether you have an accurate record of what happened (audit trail).

4. Returning the research data, such as a transcript of an interview, to the interviewee to check for accuracy of your recording (member checking).

5. Staying in the field for long periods of observation to ensure that what you observe is in fact accurate over time (prolonged engagement).

6. Testing what you find against other research or findings to ensure that your observations are accurate or that you are able to justify what you find as accurate regardless of other cases (negative case analysis).

7. Providing a detailed narrative of the research findings so that the reader of the final report would find it to be credible (thick description).

Reliability

Reliability is about the consistency of a measure, score or rating. Consider two ways in which a researcher can test for reliability:

> Two observers rate the same event, for example children's responses in a classroom to teacher threats. In a perfect world, the two observers would provide exactly the same rating or score for the same children observed. That is, reliability is perfect. This is called inter-rater reliability.

> Students write a biology test on Monday and a biology retest (the same test) on Friday. In a perfect world (for example assuming no 'practice effect'), the score of the students on Monday and Friday should be exactly the same. This is called test–retest reliability.

Since the world of research with human subjects is not perfect, researchers developed a number of techniques to estimate reliability, that is, the degree of 'error' in measurement. One such technique is called the reliability coefficient, a measure which ranges from $r = 0$ to $r = 1$ (perfect reliability). The higher the correlation coefficient (that is, the closer to 1), the higher the reliability of the measure and the lower the 'error' of measurement.

Learning points

1. Validity and reliability are two among many different criteria of scientific quality used in research.

2. Validity and reliability are understood, explained and dealt with in different ways in qualitative and quantitative research.

3. Different terminology may be used to refer to validity in quantitative and qualitative studies. For example, in qualitative studies it may be referred to as the 'trustworthiness' of the research and the 'credibility' and 'transferability' of the research findings.

4. Reliability is used more often in statistical studies and less frequently in qualitative studies, where other standards of validation are typically sought.

Describe how you will deal with validity and/or reliability issues in your research:

Validity:

Reliability:

Acknowledging the limitations of the research

ACKNOWLEDGING LIMITATIONS empowers the reader to appreciate what constraints were imposed on the study, and to understand the context in which the research claims are set.

Here is an example:

> This research on ten effective schools worked within four important limitations. First, access to schools was limited to two weeks per term by the education department. Second, three of the schools changed principals during the course of the study – with some impact on the subsequent performance of the school. Third, four of the schools could not find performance data for the preceding seven-year period. And fourth, one of the 'control' schools withdrew from the study at a late stage in the research process. The research design was adjusted accordingly, as set out in the methodology section.

Learning points

1. All studies work within limitations, for example access, time, resources, availability, and credibility of secondary data (such as departmental statistics on schools).

2. The researcher must, as far as possible, indicate how they accommodated these limitations in the study; that is, specify what trade-offs were made in the study, given the identified constraints.

3. Note that some constraints are more serious than others, and may require radical decisions (for example, changing the focus of the research) or substantial adjustments in the research design.

4. It is normally not acceptable to state limitations that indicate a lack of time or resources on the part of a researcher.

5. Some methods or methodologies have specific goals – such as depth versus breadth – and therefore cannot be considered to be limitations. For example, the inability to generalise from a case study cannot be considered a limitation of a case study, just as a survey does not typically provide in-depth knowledge on a particular issue.

Outline the constraints which you anticipate in your research *and* indicate how you would go about addressing such constraints in your study:

Limitations of the study:

Section 11

Protecting human subjects (ethics)

ETHICS is about doing the right thing. Ethics in research is about:

- protecting human subjects, that is, those involved in or affected by your research, to ensure that no harm is done in conducting or reporting your research

- protecting the integrity of your research by your actions and honesty as a researcher.

1. Consider the following two research plans, both of which involve face-to-face interviews with the participants:

> I will be conducting research to determine the attitudes of male migrant labourers in Khumalo Hostel towards HIV/AIDS.

> I plan to research the experiences of woman teachers who encountered sexual harassment in their schools.

- What do you see as the potential risks to the participants (human subjects) in these two studies?

- What specific actions could you as the researcher take to minimise the risks to participants in each of the two studies?

2. Consider the following ethical challenge:

> The funders of your research agree to fully fund your research (including international conference attendance and research assistants), provided you modify your sample. You have been unsuccessful is getting your research proposal funded. This is your final chance to undertake this research, which on completion has the potential to be significant for your career trajectory.

- Should you agree to modify your sample, what risks does this present to you as a researcher and to the integrity of your research? You suspect that the adjustment to the sample is likely to skew your research findings.

- Speculate on possible responses to the funder as well as their consequences. For example, you agree to make the changes provided this is kept confidential and more funds are provided to increase the sample size; you report the funders to the appropriate professional body; or you leak this information to the media.

Learning points

1. There are four common strategies used by researchers to protect human subjects:

    - Informed consent – this means giving the participants full information about the research, including the purpose of the research, how the results will be used, how the findings might impact on them, and where the funding for the research comes from

    - Anonymity – this means assuring the participants that their identities will not be made known

    - Confidentiality – this means that no personal information about the participants will be made available

    - Withdrawal – this means the right of the participants to withdraw from the study at any point in the process, for example during the interview.

2. Higher education institutions and many other organisations (such as the department of health overseeing clinics or the department of education responsible for schools) typically require that a researcher obtain ethical clearance before proceeding with their research.

3. Research proposals are usually evaluated for both their academic merits and for ethical clearance. The latter refers to an assessment of all aspects of the research plan, research processes and instruments (for example survey questionnaires, interview or observation schedules), including the questions to be posed to research participants.

4. It is good ethical conduct for researchers to declare any conflicts of interest. This includes any relationships with funders, research participants, etc.

Ethical conundrum

Consider the unexpected ethical dilemma in the following:

> **Research question:** How do teachers use the new science textbooks in the classroom?
>
> In the course of your observations of one teacher's classroom, you see the teacher inflicting corporal punishment on learners who did not have their textbooks with them in class.

- Should you report the teacher given that such punishment is illegal? What about your pledge in writing that personal information about the teacher as a participant in your research will remain confidential?

Application to your research

Now briefly describe what specific steps you would take to protect human subjects in your own research:

_____

_____

_____

_____

_____

_____

_____

Section 12
Estimating the budget

Research budgets are often required in research proposals as part of the process of planning to conduct the study.

Consider the costs for the study on teachers' use of the new science textbook in three schools, which involves recorded interviews with two teachers at each school, before and after their lessons.

Example of cost items include:

- Travel to 3 schools for 2 interviews per teacher (6 teachers)

- Video/Audio recording equipment and batteries

- Transcription of interview recordings (software)

- Copies of the science textbooks (3).

- What other costs might you anticipate for this study?

Learning points

1. Be as accurate and as detailed as possible in estimating costs for your research. Substantial over- or under-estimating of research costs can impact your request for funding negatively.

2. Establish what costs are allowed from the institution or agency to which you will be submitting your research proposals. For example, some funders permit purchase of research books, conference attendance, etc, while others may not.

3. Funders of research consider both the viability of the research and the costs set out for the research according to their particular criteria and overall available budget. To ensure your budget is realistic and likely to be favourably considered, find out the maximum or typical awards made by the fund being applied to before making an application.

Application to your research

Estimate the costs for your research by developing a budget for enacting your research plan.

Final thoughts

Research can be a frustrating but also an exciting process. Here are some final thoughts to encourage you on your research journey:

1. The only way to do research is to actually *do it.*

2. The most important step in research is the *quality of the research question.*

3. The most important justification for your research is its *intellectual significance*; that is, how your research advances knowledge, even modestly, in your field of study.

4. The best researchers read broadly and deeply on the topic of study. Become 'the expert' on what is known from the research literature on your chosen question.

5. The best research depends on *quality supervision*. Choose the best supervisor you can find.

6. There will always be more interesting research problems than you have time for. You have to *choose a problem* and get on with it.

7. It is completely normal to receive *critical feedback* on your research. Do not take this personally but use the feedback to improve your research.

8. The *final product* (a thesis or dissertation) will look very different from what you planned on paper in your research proposal. This is usual.

9. There will be times that you think of giving up. *Do not give up*. This is a common experience to many new researchers.

10. There are few things more *rewarding* than finishing and even publishing your research. It is worth the effort.

Further reading

This manual offers an easy-to-use, step-by-step outline for preparing your research proposal and doing research from start to finish. For more detailed information on each element of the research process, consult the following reference books.

Cohen, L, Manion, L & Morrison, K. 2018. *Research Methods in Education*. 8th ed. Routledge: New York.

Bloomberg, LD & Volpe, M. 2016. *Completing your qualitative dissertation: A road map from beginning to end*. SAGE Publications: Thousand Oaks.

Du Preez, P & Simmonds, S (eds). 2019. *A scholarship of doctoral education: On becoming a researcher*. SUN Media: Cape Town.

Galvan, JL & Galvan, MC. 2017. *Writing literature reviews: A guide for students of the social and behavioral sciences*. Routledge: New York.

Maree, JG (ed). 2016. *First steps in research*. 2nd ed. Van Schaik: Pretoria.

Miles, MB, Huberman, MA & Saldana, J. 2014. *Qualitative data analysis: A methods sourcebook*. 3rd ed. SAGE Publications: Thousand Oaks.

Mouton, J. 2014. *How to succeed in your Master's and doctoral studies: a South African guide and resource book*. 20th impression. Van Schaik: Pretoria.

Quintin, S & Reynolds, N. 2018. *Understanding research in the digital age*. SAGE Publications: Thousand Oaks.

# Web links/resources

Information gateways

SOSIG – Social science information gateway: http://sosig.ac.uk/

YENZA! – humanities and social sciences: http://www.nrf.ac.za/yenza/

Virtual libraries

IPL – Internet Public Library: http://www.ipl.org/

South African-based search engine

ANANZI: http://www.ananzi.com/

Proposal writing

National Research Foundation:

http://www.nrf.ac.za/methods/proposals.htm

http://www.nrf.ac.za/methods/reviews.htm

http://www.nrf.ac.za/methods/guide.htm

Przeworski, A & Salomon, F. 1995. revised. *The art of writing proposals: Some candid suggestions for applicants to social science research council competitions.* https://www.ssrc.org/publications/view/7A9CB4F4-815F-DE11-BD80-001CC477EC70/ (accessed 15 November 2018).

Workbooks and academic resources for postgraduate programmes

The Cape Town-based Centre for Research and Academic Development: http://www.radct.co.za

Appendix A

A.1 Reasons for 'weak' statements of purpose

1. The statement of purpose should not anticipate the outcome(s) of the research.

2. Phrases such as 'to visit' are vague and do not imply a rigorous and systematic process of inquiry. They provide no indication of 'how' or 'what' the researcher will be focusing on in the study.

3. Statements indicating the focus of the study must be written clearly and concisely and separated from the specific critical research questions and other detailed descriptions of the subjects and methodology.

A.2 Reasons for 'good' statements of purpose

In the given statements of purpose, the following aspects are common features:

1. The intention of the researcher is explicitly stated – to assess; to measure; to explore; to document; or to compare. That is, the focus statement points towards 'how' the study will be undertaken – a likely research methodological orientation is hinted at.

2. The 'object/s' of the study is/are identified – the new history curriculum; social rates of return; experiences of women executives; suicides; or how science is taught. Exactly 'what' the researcher will be focusing on is clarified.

3. The participants or subjects in the study are described – learners taught by underqualified teachers; student survivors; women executives; or novice and experienced teachers. 'Who' will be involved in the study is indicated in each statement.

4. The context/s in which the study is located is/are included or implied in the statement of purpose – primary schools; higher education; high-tech industries; campuses; or under-resourced classrooms. The focus includes a reference to the question of 'where', or what the 'sites' of, the study is/are likely to be.

5. Although the statement of purpose should be as succinct as possible, it should also convey sufficient information to allow the reader to immediately understand what the research is about.

# Appendix B

Examples of different types of research instruments follow:

B.1 Observation schedule (using categories)

    B. 1.1 Observation of teaching

    B. 1.2 Observation of learning

B.2 Observation record (using narrative)

B.3 School resource profile

B.4 Classroom environment and resource checklist

B.5 Interview schedule

B.6 Questionnaire

B.1 Observation schedule (using categories)

B. 1.1 Observation of teaching

CHANGES IN TEACHING

Indicator: Effective teachers use multiple teaching strategies

Critical question: Do teachers use multiple teaching strategies?

Criteria	Frequency (%)				
	0	1–25	26–50	51–75	76–100
lecture	☐	☐	☐	☐	☐
role play	☐	☐	☐	☐	☐
independent desk work	☐	☐	☐	☐	☐
demonstration	☐	☐	☐	☐	☐
multimedia presentation	☐	☐	☐	☐	☐
other	☐	☐	☐	☐	☐

Elaboration (record any relevant information; clarification, puzzles, elaborations)

_____

_____

_____

_____

_____

_____

_____

_____

_____

_____

_____

_____

_____

B. 1.2 Observation of learning

CHANGES IN LEARNING

Indicator: In effective classrooms students participate actively in the lessons

Critical question: Are students actively engaged in the lesson?

Criteria	Frequency		
	1	2	3
students ask questions	☐	☐	☐
students listen attentively	☐	☐	☐
students are involved in the set tasks	☐	☐	☐

Coding   1 = not at all
2 = some of the time
3 = often

Elaboration (include other relevant criteria)

B.2 Observation record (using narrative)

NARRATIVE SCHEDULE

Example

Class: Grade 7 Science
Teacher: Ms Nxumalo (coded)
School: Sunset Primary
Lesson: Acids and Bases
Date: 12 July 1995

Narrative

The teacher started the lesson about five minutes late. Apparently, she was delayed in the principal's office. She took about another ten minutes with routine administrative tasks which included the collection of homework, announcing the test date and the relevant pages to study. She constantly interrupted her announcements with appeals to students to remain quiet, return to their seats and take out their books.

After 15 minutes the lesson started. Ms Nxumalo wrote a definition for Acids on the board, which she copied from the textbook she was holding. Students were asked to repeat the definition in chorus … three times. She then called on individual students to repeat the definition by reading it off the board. She erased the definition and asked students to recall the definition. Few students could repeat the definition word for word; students laughed loudly when a fellow student struggled to get the wording right. The teacher then repeated the definition – by reading it from the textbook. This activity took about 20 minutes.

She then told the students to read quietly from the section on 'Acids and Bases' in the textbook. I noticed about four or five students sharing one textbook. I also noticed that several textbooks were in a poor state, with pages missing, covers torn and pen writing across the pages. About two minutes into this exercise, the bell rang. Students rushed towards the door. The teacher walked over to me and confided: 'This is my worst class.'

Reflections

Much time was wasted in administrative and disciplinary tasks. Teacher appeared confident but authoritarian. No questions exchanged. Students were simply instructed to repeat a definition by rote. The lesson was poorly organised. Teacher-centred lesson; lecture dominated. No visible support or display materials in the classroom related to science or to the topic for the day. No clear patterns were discernible with regard to race, gender or class discrimination.

Learning points

1. This is an abbreviated narrative for purposes of illustration only. You may have a longer narrative.

2. You need not record everything that happens in the classroom – only the main sequence of events during the period relevant to your research question(s).

3. We would encourage the occasional use of direct, selected quotations of teacher/student talk, especially if they add powerfully to the broad focal questions of interest in the classroom observations.

B.3 School resource profile

1. **What is the general condition of your school buildings?**

1.1	the school needs complete rebuilding
1.2	some classrooms need major repairs
1.3	most or all classrooms need minor repairs
1.4	some classrooms need minor repairs
1.5	in good condition

2. **Which of the following does your school have, and in what condition?**

		Yes	No	Good	Poor
2.1	school library				
2.2	school hall				
2.3	store room				
2.4	staff room				
2.5	sports field				
2.6	separate office for principal				
2.7	separate office for school secretary				
2.8	telephone				
2.9	fax machine				
2.10	photocopier				
2.11	computer				
2.12	overhead projector				
2.13	data projector				
2.14	radio				
2.15	electricity				
2.16	piped water				
2.17	science laboratory				
2.18	toilets				

3. **Which of the following are found in the classrooms of your school?**

	All	Most	Some	None
3.1 a usable chalkboard				
3.2 chalk				
3.3 a cupboard				
3.4 a teacher table				
3.5 a teacher chair				
3.6 a wall chart of any kind				
3.7 student desks				
3.8 other				

Comment

4. **Which statement most accurately depicts the general availability of textbooks in your school? The approximate percentage of students who have all the required textbooks in all school subjects is:**

4.1 about 90–100

4.2 about 75–89

4.3 about 50–74

4.4 about 25–49

4.5 about 0–24

B.4 Classroom environment and resource checklist

School name ....

School size (number of pupils) ....

School type (for example, farm; primary) ....

Teacher's name ....

CLASSROOM ENVIRONMENT

Tick 'Yes' or 'No'. Please give details where necessary.

	Yes	No	Details
1. Adequate desks for all students			
2. Table for teacher			
3. Room is quiet			
4. Lighting is adequate			
5. Adequate space for movement around classroom			
6. Classroom is cheerful and inviting			
7. Ventilation/temperature is comfortable			

Comment

....

....

....

RESOURCES CHECKLIST

V = Visible in classroom but not used.   U = Used this period.   N = Not visible.
Please indicate by putting a circle around the relevant letter. If not sure, check with the teacher.

1. Comic books	V	U	N
2. Comic workbooks	V	U	N
3. Textbooks	V	U	N
4. Exercise books	V	U	N
5. Overhead projector	V	U	N
6. Audio tapes	V	U	N
7. Audio tape player	V	U	N
8. Wallcharts	V	U	N
9. Television and video player	V	U	N
10. Power points	V	U	N
11. Chalkboard and chalk	V	U	N
12. Others (pens; scissors; paper)	V	U	N

Comment

....

....

B.5 Interview schedule

SCHEDULE FOR FOLLOW-UP INTERVIEW WITH TEACHER
AFTER S/HE HAS USED THE MATERIAL IN CLASS

What do teachers use and value in the new materials?

1. How did you feel introducing this new material to the children?

2. Did the comic help you cover the key science concepts in the syllabus topic?

3. What can you say about your pupils' response to the comic?

   checklist:

   - enjoyment

   - excitement

   - boredom

   - understanding

   - confusion

   - participation.

4. Do you think that this comic can help children learn? What did they learn? How did they learn it?

5. Have you learnt anything new from using the comic with your class?

How do teachers use the materials in different contexts?

6. Did you have all the comics that you needed?

7. Do you feel that you used the comic in the way that you intended?

8. What preparation did you have to do?

9. In what ways can the comic help teachers to improve their teaching?

What support do teachers need to use the materials?

10. Did the training with the comic give you new ideas about teaching and the use of new materials?

11. Do you need any further support to use the material? If so, what support do you need?

B.6 Questionnaire

EVALUATION PRACTICE (EP) READER SURVEY

Currently, content for EP is divided among the sections listed in a–j below. How important is each of those sections? Please circle the numeral that best reflects your response, using the scale below. Then, please check how you *most typically* approach each of these sections. (We recognise that this will vary with topic, etc, but we are after your *typical* use of each section.)

I feel strongly that this section SHOULD NOT be included		I am NEUTRAL about whether this section is included		I feel strongly that this section SHOULD be included
1	2	3	4	5

In approaching this section, I *typically*:

								Skip it	Scan it	Read it
a)	Articles	1	2	3	4	5				
b)	Forum (essays, opinions and professional judgements addressing the philosophical and ethical dilemmas of the evaluation professions)	1	2	3	4	5				
c)	In Response (concise comments from readers regarding articles previously published in EP)	1	2	3	4	5				
d)	Interviews and Panel Discussions (discussions with important stakeholders or those with views of general interest to evaluators)	1	2	3	4	5				
e)	Book Reviews	1	2	3	4	5				
f)	Traces (excerpts from previously published articles, books or speeches which influenced the profession)	1	2	3	4	5				
g)	Tools, Products and Services (new items – or old items used in new ways – that might interest practising evaluators)	1	2	3	4	5				
h)	Recent Evaluations (lists of reviews of recently published articles or reports of actual evaluations)	1	2	3	4	5				
i)	Letters to the Editor	1	2	3	4	5				
j)	'News' (enclosed with each EP mailing)	1	2	3	4	5				

Notes:

 # Other research titles available from Juta

Assignment and Thesis Writing

South African edition

J Anderson & M Poole

978 0 70217 748 4

978 0 70219 640 9

2009

192 PAGES

'This edition provides the tools and insights necessary to write succinctly and logically, to complete theses and essays in time, to comply with standards of academic scholarship, to conduct in-depth research and to develop general writing and computer skills and proficiency.' Professor Nqabomzi Gawe, Deputy Vice-Chancellor: Institutional Support, Durban University of Technology.

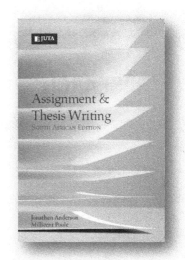

Growing the next generation of researchers

A handbook for emerging researchers and their mentors

L Holness

978 1 77582 085 7

978 1 77582 197 7

2015

280 PAGES

Designed as a tool for emerging researchers and their mentors, this book provides strategies for research growth in areas such as understanding the relationship between teaching and research; obtaining higher degrees; producing peer-reviewed research output; generating and managing research funding; effective research planning; engaging in interdisciplinary research; and postgraduate supervision. It addresses

three primary readerships: institutions, mentors of new or inexperienced academics and emerging researchers themselves. It is set in an African context, addressing topics and challenges relevant across the continent.

Marketing Research

J Wiid & C Diggines (Editors)

978 1 48511 200 6

978 1 48511 548 9

3e 2015

360 PAGES

Marketing Research, now in its third edition, provides a methodical introduction to the basic concepts of marketing research.

Marketing research can be a daunting subject if not taught correctly. The mere mention of inferential statistics or statistical significance causes many students to close their minds and develop a mental block towards the topic. This is largely because most texts spend too little time teaching students the basic concepts before ploughing into the analysis of data and associated statistical formulas.

Marketing Research follows a simple layout that is easy to read with text that is written in understandable, plain English. It will equip undergraduate marketing students with the skills necessary to plan and conduct basic marketing research projects in an efficient and effective manner, in a business world which demands more and more information on which to base decisions.

Research Matters

F du Plooy-Cilliers, C Davis & RM Bezuidenhout (Editors)

978 1 48510 201 4

978 1 48510 433 9

2014

352 PAGES

Research Matters is a text written for South African undergraduate students. It diffuses typically dense content into easy-to-read chapters to guide beginners through each step in the research process. Examples and applications used in the text focus on research problems and objectives in South Africa which students can identify with.